SAM HOLCROFT

Sam Holcroft's plays include *The Wardrobe*, commissioned as part of the 2014 National Theatre Connections Festival; *Edgar & Annabel*, part of the *Double Feature* season at the Paintframe, at the National Theatre, London; *Dancing Bears*, part of the *Charged* season for Clean Break at Soho Theatre and Latitude Festival; *While You Lie* at the Traverse, Edinburgh; *Pink*, part of the *Women, Power and Politics* season at the Tricycle; *Vanya*, adapted from Chekhov, at The Gate; *Cockroach*, co-produced by the National Theatre of Scotland and Traverse (nominated for Best New Play 2008, by the Critics' Awards for Theatre in Scotland and shortlisted for the John Whiting Award, 2009) and *Ned and Sharon* at the HighTide Festival. Sam received the Tom Erhardt Award in 2009, was the Pearson Writer-in-Residence at the Traverse Theatre, 2009–10, and was appointed Writer-in-Residence at the National Theatre Studio in 2013.

Sam Holcroft

COCKROACH

NICK HERN BOOKS
London
www.nickhernbooks.co.uk

A Nick Hern Book

Cockroach first published in Great Britain as a paperback original in 2008 by Nick Hern Books Limited, The Glasshouse, 49a Goldhawk Road, London W12 8QP, in association with the National Theatre of Scotland and the Traverse Theatre, Edinburgh

Reprinted 2014

Cockroach copyright © 2008 Sam Holcroft

Sam Holcroft has asserted her right to be identified as the author of this work

Cover image: Pakmor
Cover design: Ned Hoste, 2H

Typeset by Nick Hern Books, London
Printed in Great Britain by Mimeo Ltd, Cambridgeshire PE29 6XX

A CIP catalogue record for this book is available from the British Library

ISBN   978 1 84842 032 8

Cockroach was first performed at the Traverse Theatre, Edinburgh, on 23 October 2008, as part of their *Traverse Debuts* season. The cast was as follows:

MMOMA	Frances Ashman
DAVEY	Ryan Fletcher
BETH	Meg Fraser
DANIELLE	Laura McMonagle
LEAH	Helen Mallon
LEE	Owen Whitelaw
Director	Vicky Featherstone
Designer	Naomi Wilkinson
Lighting Designer	Lizzie Powell
Sound Designer	Matthew Padden

Characters

LEE
LEAH
DANIELLE
MMOMA
DAVEY
BETH, *their teacher*

Thanks

Thanks to Mel Kenyon, Kirsty Coombs, Vicky Featherstone,
Dominic Hill and all at the National Theatre of Scotland and the
Traverse Theatre. And my family, Elizabeth Humphreys and
Emily Lowe.

S.H.

A classroom.

The stage is bare but for desks, a door and a window.

The stage is in darkness.

The door slams.

The light opens on LEE.

LEE (*shouts*). Leah.

> LEE *bangs on the door.*

> Open the door.

> LEE *bangs harder.*

> Leah, open the fucking door.

> *The light extends to* LEAH *on the other side of the door.*

LEAH. Go away.

LEE. Let me in.

LEAH. Stay. Away from me –

LEE. Let. Me in.

LEAH. You.

LEE. Open up.

LEAH. You.

LEE. Open up this –

LEAH. Cunt.

> *Beat.*

> I hate you.

LEE. She was nothing to me.

LEAH. I *hate* you.

LEE. *Nothing* to me.

Less than nothing: nobody.

She is dead to me, Leah.

Dead.

Beat.

LEAH. I never want to see you again.

LEE *throws himself at the door.*

Lee, stop it!

The wood splinters.

Stop it, Lee, you're breaking the door!

LEAH *backs into the classroom.*

LEE *hurls himself at the door again and again.*

DANIELLE *enters.*

DANIELLE. Leah? Leah, you in there?

LEAH. Danielle? Danielle, help! Help me!

DANIELLE *runs off.*

LEE *continues to throw himself at the door.*

LEAH *goes to the window and tries to open it.*

Somebody help me, please!

DANIELLE *comes running back in with their science teacher,* BETH.

BETH. Lee! Lee, stop it!

DANIELLE. Stop it, Lee!

LEE *thrashes about and almost hits* BETH. *She reels backwards.*

Miss? You all right?

BETH. Stand back, Danielle.

Lee. Stop this now. Do you want me to call for help?

LEE *ignores her.*

You're getting yourself into a lot of trouble, Lee. The longer you continue, the worse it will be. You remember the last time you did this, Lee.

LEE *bangs the door in frustration.*

Lee, if you show me that you're listening to me then that will improve your situation right now.

Lee!

LEE *continues to beat the door.*

Not only are you now in trouble for the original offence, Lee, but now you are not following a teacher's instructions. I'm going to have to call for help.

BETH *raises her walkie-talkie to her mouth.*

LEE *tears himself away from the door.*

BETH *lowers the walkie-talkie.*

Well done. Well done, Lee; that was the right thing to do. That was the right choice. Thank you for listening to me.

LEE *thrashes about.*

Now you're to stand still there. Right there, Lee, then we're going to go straight to Referral Base, okay? You know what will happen if you don't stand still there. Don't make this any worse for yourself. I don't want to hear a word from you. Understood?

LEE *is silent.*

Thank you.

BETH *raises her walkie-talkie to her mouth and patches in.*

W11C to Referral Base, receiving?

'Karen, receiving' is heard back over the walkie-talkie.

I'll be coming down from the Science Corridor to Referral Base with Lee Donegal, 11C. Can you have someone to meet us please?

'Got it, on standby at Referral Base' is heard back over the walkie-talkie.

BETH *fits her walkie-talkie back into its holster on her hip.*

She motions to LEE *to stay where he is. She takes a key from her pocket and unlocks the shattered door. She steps inside.* DANIELLE *follows.*

DANIELLE. Leah?

LEAH. It weren't my fault, Miss. I didn't do nothing.

BETH. Are you all right?

LEAH. It weren't my fault. It were that bitch, Mmoma.

BETH. How did you lock this door, Leah?

LEAH. I don't know, Miss.

BETH. Give me the key.

LEAH. I don't have a key, Miss.

BETH. Give me the key, Leah.

LEAH *takes the key out of her pocket and hands it to* BETH.

What is going on here?

LEAH. I told you, it weren't my fault. I was trying to get away from him. (*Raises her voice so* LEE *can hear.*) Protect myself. I was only trying to take myself out of harm's way.

DANIELLE. He was going to come in here, Miss –

LEAH (*pointing*). He was going to come in here and...

The window smashes and something flies into the room.

The girls scream.

BETH. Everybody get down! Get down. Now, get on the floor!

The girls fall to the floor.

LEE *flees in the commotion.*

Stay down, girls. Stay. Down. Is everyone okay?

Are you okay?

Stay on the floor.

BETH *moves around on her belly until she finds the offending article, a ball.*

She stands and marches to the window and looks down into the playground.

Davey! David Lowe, you come up here now. Now. Davey...

You girls stay here. Don't touch the glass or the wood. Just stay where you are.

LEAH. On the floor, Miss?

BETH. No, get up, everybody get up. Are you hurt?

LEAH. No.

BETH. Is anyone hurt?

ALL. No.

BETH. Good okay. Stay where you are.

BETH *exits the classroom and sees that* LEE *is gone.*

Lee? Lee!

BETH *unholsters her walkie-talkie and raises it to her mouth, she patches in.*

(*As she walks back down the corridor and off.*) W11C to Referral Base, receiving?

'Karen, receiving' is heard back over the walkie-talkie.

We have a broken window and door in classroom W11C on the Science Corridor, Lee Donegal has fled the scene and David Lowe should be on his way up from the playground. Can we get a search out for Lee Donegal, please? He is not to leave school grounds.

'Got it' is heard back over the static.

LEAH and DANIELLE *remain in the classroom. They brush themselves off.*

MMOMA *enters and walks down the corridor. She walks past the classroom,* LEAH *clocks her.*

LEAH. Mmoma! Bitch!

MMOMA *spins on her heels.*

You bitch-whore, get back here!

LEAH *races out and pulls* MMOMA *back into the classroom.* MMOMA *struggles out of her grip. They face each other.*

Skank.

LEAH *spits on the ground in front of* MMOMA*'s feet.*

MMOMA. I didn't know he was your boyfriend.

LEAH. Everybody knows he's my boyfriend.

MMOMA. *I* didn't know.

LEAH. *You* are a liar.

MMOMA. Why would I want *your* boyfriend?

LEAH. What are you saying?

MMOMA. I want my *own* boyfriend.

LEAH. Liar! You're just lying right to my face.

You are boyfriend-stealing, lying little whore.

MMOMA. I am not.

LEAH. Yes you are. That's what you are. That is exactly what you are.

MMOMA. That's not what I am.

LEAH. You're nothing. He said that, you know?

He said you were dead to him.

Dead.

Beat.

MMOMA. Then what are you?

What are you then if he'd cheat on you with a corpse?

LEAH *goes for her. They scrap amongst the glass and splintered wood, biting and scratching and kicking. With the help of* DANIELLE, LEAH *pins* MMOMA *to a desk and pulls a clump of hair extensions out of her head. She stands back holding them triumphantly aloft.*

LEAH. Look at that. Look at the whore's fake hair.

What are these? Pubes?

MMOMA *breaks free of* DANIELLE*'s grip and launches herself at* LEAH. *They struggle in front of the window until* MMOMA *grabs a thick shard of glass and presses it against* LEAH*'s neck. They all freeze.* MMOMA *looks down at the glass pricking blood from* LEAH*'s neck. She drops the glass. She staggers back.*

BETH *can be heard coming down the corridor with* DAVEY.

DAVEY. But, Miss –

BETH. Davey, you will look at this broken window and you will see what you have done.

DAVEY. But it were an accident, Miss! I didn't do it on purpose.

BETH *enters the classroom with* DAVEY.

BETH. It's about taking responsibility for your actions, accident or not.

BETH *sees the girls in disarray,* MMOMA*'s hair on the floor. She tries to catch her breath.*

DAVEY. We were just playing, Miss. No harm meant.

LEE *creeps back down the corridor towards the classroom and tries to get* LEAH*'s attention.*

It were just a ball, Miss.

What did you think?

Did you think –

BETH (*shouting over* DAVEY *to the girls*). What are you, a bag of cats?

The girls look at the floor.

BETH *tries to catch her breath.*

LEE (*whispers*). Pst. Leah?

BETH *walks her desk and opens her handbag.*

BETH. This is not acceptable.

All of you are in a lot of trouble.

There is uproar.

BETH *pulls an asthma inhaler out of her handbag.*

Be quiet!

And don't think I can't see you out there, Lee Donegal.

LEE *turns to scarper.*

And you know full well that if you run away again you're only going to make it worse for yourself. Now get in my classroom, please.

LEE *moves into the room.*

BETH *sucks on her inhaler.*

LEAH. Miss –

BETH *holds up her hand to silence them all.*

They all wait the obligatory ten seconds in silence.

BETH *breathes out.*

BETH. You are all in detention for the foreseeable future.

Again there is uproar.

BETH *holds up her hand.*

And you won't be sitting here doing nothing, no sir, you will learn.

This is not a farm.

You are not farm animals.

This is a school.

This is my classroom and you will learn from me.

You will have knowledge.

The light narrows on BETH.

And you will succeed.

BETH *sinks into her chair.*

She pulls off her comfortable shoes and puts on a pair of high heels.

She stands to go.

The light closes on BETH *and opens on* DANIELLE.

DANIELLE *sits eating a sandwich out of cling film at her desk.*

The light extends to DAVEY.

DAVEY. All right, Danielle.

   Startled, DANIELLE *tries to cover her sandwiches with her hands.*

DANIELLE. Oh, hi Davey.

   DAVEY *stands awkwardly.*

DAVEY. I forgot my bag.

   Beat.

   DAVEY *crosses to get his bag.*

   DANIELLE *picks grime off the desk. She looks up at him.*

   He stands with his bag.

DANIELLE. You got it then?

DAVEY. Yeah.

DAVEY *pats his bag.*

DANIELLE *turns back to the desk, she tries to subtly brush crumbs off her face.*

DAVEY *stands awkwardly.*

DAVEY. So. So how's it going, then?

DANIELLE *looks up.*

DANIELLE. Oh yeah, all right, yeah.

DAVEY. What you doing?

DANIELLE. Oh nothing.

DAVEY. You having some sandwiches?

DANIELLE. Oh yeah, right.

DAVEY. What sort of sandwiches you got?

DANIELLE. Just. You know, just sandwiches.

DAVEY. You got nothing in them?

DANIELLE. In them?

DAVEY. In your sandwiches, there nothing in your sandwiches?

DANIELLE. Oh right, no there is, yeah.

DAVEY. What?

DANIELLE. Egg. There's egg in my sandwiches. I know most people don't like egg, but I like egg.

DAVEY. I like egg. I like egg in my sandwiches.

DANIELLE. Do you?

DAVEY. Yeah, I do, yeah.

DANIELLE. Oh right.

DANIELLE *smiles, relieved.*

Beat.

D'you want one?

DAVEY. What?

DANIELLE. D'you want a sandwich?

DAVEY. Me?

DANIELLE. Yeah.

Beat. They look at one another. DAVEY *can't believe his luck.*

DAVEY. Yeah.

DANIELLE *smiles and hands him a sandwich. He eats standing up. He wolfs it down in a few mouthfuls.*

DANIELLE. It's not much.

DAVEY. It's great.

DANIELLE. It was only small.

DAVEY (*overly enthusiastic*). No, it was great.

DANIELLE. Thanks.

Pause.

D'you want mine?

DAVEY. What? No, no, it's yours.

DANIELLE. I don't mind.

DAVEY. I can't eat your sandwich.

DANIELLE. I'm not hungry, really.

DAVEY. Are you sure?

DANIELLE. Yeah, really, I'm not hungry.

She offers it to him with a smile. He takes it. He eats.

DAVEY. So did you not finish these at lunch?

DANIELLE. No, these are my dinner.

DAVEY *stops eating.*

DAVEY. What, this is your dinner? Danielle, you should have told me – I can't eat your dinner.

DANIELLE. It's all right, I told you, I'm not hungry.

DAVEY. D'you always eat your dinner at school?

DANIELLE. Yes.

DAVEY. You don't go home for your dinner?

DANIELLE. No.

DAVEY. Why d'you not go home for your dinner?

Beat.

You live with your mum, right?

DANIELLE. My stepdad too.

DAVEY. Why don't you want to go home?

DANIELLE. I got some chewing gum.

DAVEY. What?

DANIELLE. D'you want some?

DAVEY. Oh right, yeah, thanks, gets rid of the…

DANIELLE. Egg.

DAVEY. Yeah.

DANIELLE *rummages in her bag for the chewing gum.*

DANIELLE. D'you want to sit down?

Beat.

DAVEY. Yeah.

DAVEY *takes a seat, she passes him a stick of gum. They chew on their gum.*

Silence.

You know Mark?

DANIELLE. Who?

DAVEY. Mark Chatters. Lives on Lee's estate. You know the one.

DANIELLE. What, Frankie's Mark?

DAVEY. Yeah, he's the one with the monkey.

DANIELLE. Monkey?

DAVEY. Yeah, he's got a monkey, like, illegally.

DANIELLE. No. I didn't know.

DAVEY. Well, he has. And get this. He came home last week and found it up on the sofa shagging the cat.

DANIELLE. What?

DAVEY (*imitating*). Yeah, the monkey's up on the sofa giving it to the cat.

DAVEY *laughs*.

DANIELLE. That's disgusting. Why are you telling me this?

DAVEY. Sorry, I thought you'd find it funny. The guys thought it was funny, sorry; I didn't mean to upset you. You're right, it's not funny, sorry, it's not funny at all. I was just trying to make you laugh. Sorry, Danielle, I just wanted you to laugh. You got a great laugh.

DANIELLE. No.

DAVEY. You do.

DANIELLE. I don't.

DAVEY. You do, Danielle, you do. It's magic.

She looks at him.

DAVEY *braces himself*.

I love. It when you laugh in class. When you do, you light it up. All that shite. Becomes bearable. And you are all I hear. But I wish it was me, though, that was making you laugh. I wish it was me.

Beat.

You're well fit, Danielle.

Beat.

I mean. Sorry. Shit, I mean. You're pretty.

I think you're pretty.

Beautiful.

Sorry.

DANIELLE. That's all right.

DAVEY. Sorry.

DANIELLE. Thanks.

DAVEY. Can I kiss you? I really want to kiss you.

DANIELLE *smiles at him.*

DAVEY *leans across the table and kisses her. He pulls back.*

Beat.

DAVEY. Thanks.

DANIELLE *smiles bashfully.*

I've got to go.

DANIELLE. You do?

DAVEY. Yeah. I should get back, my mum…

DANIELLE. Yeah. Right.

DAVEY. You going to go home?

DANIELLE. No. Not yet.

DAVEY. When you going to go home, Danielle?

DANIELLE. I'll see you tomorrow.

DAVEY. Yeah. See ya.

DAVEY *slings his bag onto his shoulder and goes.*

DANIELLE *smoothes the ball of cling film out onto the desk. When it is flat she suddenly pulls it taut over her face. She sucks in air in an attempt to suffocate herself. She struggles for several seconds before ripping the cling film away.*

The light narrows on DANIELLE *gulping in air.*

The light closes on DANIELLE *and opens on* LEAH *and* LEE.

LEAH. Lee.

LEE *ignores her.*

Fuck's sake, Lee.

LEE *ignores her still.*

Look at me, Lee.

Beat.

Lee, why won't you look at me?

Don't like what you see?

The light suddenly opens onto the rest of the class.

BETH. 'Hormones in the Menstrual Cycle.'

LEAH. Lee.

BETH. Stop talking, Leah. If you can't be silent, then you're going to have to move.

'Hormones in the Menstrual Cycle.'

Together out loud: what is a hormone…?

ALL. A chemical messenger.

BETH. It travels at…?

ALL. The speed of blood.

BETH. In order to…?

ALL. Activate target cells.

BETH. Good. Lee, can you take your bag off so I know you're staying, please.

LEE *reluctantly takes off his bag.*

Now I know this is detention and there may only be five of you, but classroom rules still apply: I am going to ask you questions and you are going to answer, but I will only ask *one* person at a time and therefore only *one* person at a time will answer. That is *one* person only, do you understand? Davey, can you please take your jumper off, this may be after-school hours but you should all still be wearing regulation uniform.

DAVEY *pulls his jumper off over his head*.

Thank you. Davey, you can start us off: at what stage in the menstrual cycle does ovulation take place?

DAVEY. Dunno.

BETH. Look at the diagram, Davey, it's on the diagram.

DAVEY. Stage Four.

BETH. That's right. Stage Four. Write it down. Davey if you don't write it down you won't remember it that's why you don't remember it Davey because you haven't written it down before write it down Davey: 'Stage Four, Day Fourteen, the egg is released.' Can't write without a pen, Davey. Leah, can you come and sit down here please.

LEAH. What? No!

BETH. Come and sit down here.

LEAH. No, I'm not moving.

BETH. I said I wouldn't ask you again. This is a punishment, Leah, you're not supposed to be sitting here chatting. Lee, can you tell me what happens once the egg is released, please? Look at the diagram. Leah, stand up and come and sit down here.

LEAH. Danielle gets to sit next to Davey.

BETH. Danielle hasn't been talking.

LEAH. Miss, that's not fair, not when –

BETH. Right, boys on one side, girls on the other.

There is uproar.

Boys on one side. Girls on the other. We have a lot to do, your exam is in four weeks. You boys have already fallen a year behind. Do you want to throw away your chance of getting in to college? You want to throw away your chance for success?

Everybody stand up to move seats.

They reluctantly stand to move seats.

Girls on this side, boys on that side, I'm giving you five seconds to move and be sat down with your pens and papers out starting – Five. Four. Three. Two. Leah, you're not in your seat. One. Lee, what happens once the egg is released? Look at the diagram; none of you can see what I'm talking about unless you are looking at the diagram right here.

She points at the diagram.

What happens to the egg once it's released?

LEE. It's fertilised.

BETH. If it is not fertilised by Day Twenty-eight of the cycle then what happens, Danielle? Look at the diagram.

MMOMA. The lining of the womb breaks down.

BETH. Thank you, Mmoma, but I asked Danielle.

DANIELLE. So you can only get pregnant between Day Fourteen and Day Twenty-eight?

BETH. Actually it's less than that, the period of fertility is marginalised by the blocking of the cervix with vaginal mucus –

LEAH. Miss, can you not use that word, please?

DAVEY. So you can have sex all the other times and not get pregnant?

BETH. What?

DAVEY. You can have sex in all this bit of the graph, and not get pregnant?

Beat.

BETH. No.

DAVEY. But, Miss –

BETH. No. Don't have sex.

DAVEY. What?

BETH. With that in mind. It's not reliable, there are no obvious signs, there is no way of knowing for sure –

DAVEY. Why?

BETH. Can we move on, please.

DAVEY. Why's there no way of knowing? It would save a lot of trouble…

DANIELLE *looks at him.*

I mean. Not for me.

BETH. Most adult female mammals will have a way of obviously advertising that brief phase of their reproductive cycle when they are ovulating.

DAVEY. Like how, Miss?

BETH. It may be visual: the area around the vagina turns bright red.

DAVEY *laughs.*

DANIELLE *looks at him, he stops.*

LEAH. Please don't use that word, Miss.

BETH. That happens to baboons.

LEAH. I don't like that word.

LEE. Baboon's not got a pussy, Leah.

BETH. Lee. It could also be an olfactory signal. The female may give off a certain smell and it could also be behavioural. This again is true for baboons: the female will crouch down in front of the male and present him her hindquarters.

LEAH. 'Hindquarters'?

BETH. Her vagina. She would display her vagina.

LEAH. Please, Miss!

LEE. Then why don't you?

Beat.

BETH. What?

LEE. Why don't you do that? Crouch down. Show me your hindquarters.

Beat.

BETH. Interesting question, Lee; one that you could pose in an exam essay.

LEE *scoffs*.

MMOMA. How is that, Miss?

BETH. You could contrast human sexuality with the sexuality of most other mammals and you would find a great many differences. The most obvious being that most mammalian females exhibit conspicuous –

LEAH. What's conspicuous?

BETH. – obvious signs of ovulation and will only solicit sex during that brief –

LEAH. What's 'solicit'?

BETH. – that brief period. Only during that brief period will she be receptive – receive. Accept. Allow. Sex. Only during those fertile days. And she will be sexually unattractive, or at least less attractive, to the males on other days because she is not exhibiting those arousing signals. Now in contrast, in human females there are no external or significant internal clues to suggest when we. When the female might be ovulating.

LEE. So you could be ovulating, Miss.

BETH. I'm sorry?

LEE. You could be ripe, right now.

LEAH. Lee.

BETH. The human female is receptive to sex throughout the entire reproductive cycle. (*Referring to the graph.*) Through

Stage One to Four. So you say, Davey, that it would be handy to know when to avoid sex? But if that situation were true for us as a species, you would only find a woman sexually attractive for a few days of the month. You would only have sex a few days of each month.

LEE. Be more than he's getting now.

DAVEY. Fuck off, Lee.

DANIELLE. Yeah, fuck off, Lee. Just cos you've shagged half this classroom.

LEAH. Hey. What the fuck? You're my fucking friend, Danielle. Don't even speak about me in the same sentence as that (*Re:* MMOMA.) fucking monkey over there –

BETH. Hey, that's enough.

MMOMA *stands up*.

Sit down, Mmoma.

LEAH *stands up*.

Leah, sit down.

LEAH (*to* MMOMA). You want to go for it?

MMOMA. You want to go for it?

LEE *stands up, enjoying the commotion*.

BETH. Hang on a second, let's remember why we're here. Sit down.

LEAH. What?

MMOMA. What d'you mean?

BETH. Sit down, all of you. (*To* LEAH *and* MMOMA.) Let's remember why you're here.

BETH *turns to* LEE.

Lee, is there anything you want to say? (*Pause*.) Seeing as you can't discuss this without becoming animals yourselves –

LEE. Thought we was animals, Miss.

BETH. You will be doing worksheets for the rest of detention in silence.

There is uproar.

Silence!

The light narrows on BETH.

BETH *sinks into her chair.*

She pulls off her comfortable shoes and puts on her high heels.

She takes out her make-up bag and puts on some lip gloss.

She stands.

The lights extends to LEE *who has been watching her.*

Lee.

LEE. All right, Miss.

BETH. See you tomorrow, Lee.

LEE. Look nice, Miss.

Beat.

BETH *goes.*

Enjoy your evening, Miss.

LEE *boards up the door.*

LEAH *approaches.*

LEAH. They got you fixing the door?

LEE *fixes the door.*

Cunts.

Right?

LEE *fixes the door.*

Lee?

Don't they got a carpenter?

LEE. Diverting funds.

LEAH. Oh.

LEE. I can fix a door.

LEAH. Sure you can.

Beat.

LEE *fixes the door.*

Lee? Lee, why are you angry with me?

LEE. Why didn't you open the door?

Why didn't you open the door, Leah? Instead I'm out here shouting like a fucking gimp. All you needed to do was open up. Now I'm on report.

LEAH. I'm on report.

LEE. Now I'm fixing a door, Leah. Now I'm fixing the fucking door.

You should fix this door.

LEAH. All right, I'll fix it.

LEE. Go on then.

LEE *steps back and hands* LEAH *the tools. She takes them. She doesn't know where to begin. She takes a hammer and nail and tries to board the door. The board falls. She picks it up. She tries to nail it, she drops the nail. She tries again and fails.* LEE *watches.* LEAH *gives up.*

LEAH. I can't fix it, Lee.

LEE *holds out his hands and takes the tools from her. He goes back to fixing the door.*

LEAH *stands by him.*

LEAH. I'm sorry, Lee. I'm sorry I didn't open the door.

But.

You really hurt me.

LEE. Didn't you listen to me? Didn't you hear me when I said it meant nothing?

LEAH. Then why?

LEE. She came on to me. She exposed herself. Showed herself to me.

LEAH. Why d'you look?

LEE. She put herself in front of my eyes.

LEAH. Yeah, but –

LEE. – but nothing, Leah. You don't do that. You don't do that to a man. All right?

LEAH. All right, Lee. It weren't me.

LEE. No. You wouldn't do that.

LEAH. No.

LEE. I know you wouldn't.

> LEE *turns back to the door.*

LEAH. Lee?

LEE. Would you just let me fix this door.

LEAH. Come here.

LEE. I've got to fix the door.

LEAH. Please, Lee.

> LEE *fixes the door.*

> LEAH *moves to him and slips herself in front of him, between him and the door.*

Lee.

I'm frightened, Lee.

She kisses him. He kisses her back.

The light closes on them kissing hard against the shattered door.

The light opens on DANIELLE *and* MMOMA.

DANIELLE. Aaron got called.

MMOMA. What? No.

DANIELLE. Yeah, his number got called and his letter came
through last night. That's why Luke enlisted.

MMOMA. Really, is that why?

DANIELLE. Yeah, so they could go together. Luke signed up
cos he didn't want his little brother going alone.

MMOMA. Really?

DANIELLE. Well, he's not been called has he?

MMOMA. Dean signed up.

DANIELLE. Yeah, and you know who's took his place, don't
you, in midfield?

MMOMA. Who?

DANIELLE. Norman.

MMOMA. What?

DANIELLE. Exactly, Norman Fraser is playing midfield. He
walks with a limp. Nobody can really say nothing. Besides,
you know, who else is there? And if Mark goes, and Steven...
I mean, we're not going to have a football team any more.

MMOMA. We could play.

DANIELLE. Yeah right.

MMOMA. Why not?

DANIELLE. I can't play football.

The light extends to DAVEY.

DAVEY (*to* DANIELLE). I could teach you.

DANIELLE. What?

DANIELLE *gets off the desk.*

DAVEY. To play. I'm still on the team.

But you wouldn't be any good.

You weren't made for football.

Beat.

They sit together.

MMOMA *sits alone.*

The light extends to BETH.

BETH. I said, has anyone seen Leah or Lee? Does anyone know where they are? It's five past.

DAVEY. No, Miss, sorry.

BETH. Danielle?

DANIELLE. I dunno, Miss. Though she's coming from English, Miss, probably saying goodbye to everybody else who's going home, Miss.

BETH. Don't get smart with me, Danielle. You'd be going home too if you all hadn't behaved like animals in my classroom.

BETH *takes her walkie-talkie out of her holster and patches in.*

W11C to Referral Base, receiving?

I'm looking for Leah Rose and Lee Donegal. They should be on their way to detention in W11C on the Science Corridor.

Only static is heard in reply.

BETH *clicks the walkie-talkie on and off. She tries again.*

W11C to Referral Base, can you hear me? I'm looking for Leah Rose and Lee Donegal.

'Karen, receiving, no sign of them here, we'll put search out' is heard back over the static.

The light extends to LEAH *and* LEE *looking dishevelled.*

You're late.

LEAH. It weren't my fault, Miss.

BETH. Nothing's ever your fault, Leah.

LEAH. No, Miss – it's not! Candice couldn't find her shoe, yeah – I mean, what she was doing with her stinking feet out in the classroom I don't know – but I couldn't get out, Miss, because we all had to stay and look for her shoe, and then she says I took it. What would I want with her shoe?

BETH. All right, Leah, sit down.

LEAH. Asked to search my bag, Miss. Thinking I had her shoe in my bag.

BETH. Sit down, Leah.

LEAH. She wears a size eight. Does it look like I could fit a size eight in my bag? That's a canoe, Miss. Does it look like I could fit a canoe in this bag?

BETH. Sit down. And be quiet, Leah.

LEAH. I'm just saying it weren't my fault.

LEAH *goes to sit down.*

BETH. What did I say?

Girls on one side, boys on the other.

That goes for you too, Danielle. Davey. Up you get.

Quickly. We are wasting good time here.

BETH *patches in on the walkie-talkie as they all get up and reluctantly and noisily separate.*

W11C to Referral Base. Leah and Lee have arrived in class. Call off the search.

'Got it' is heard back over the static. BETH *holsters the walkie-talkie.*

Now sit down, please, everyone.

Leah, sit down, please. Next chapter: 'Natural Selection', page eighty-six, please head your revision with the title 'Natural Selection'. Lee, you can't write if you don't have a pen. Please find a pen. Davey, take your jumper off. If I see it again, you won't see it again, all right?

DAVEY *pulls his jumper off over his head.*

Thank you.

Lee, I said please find a pen.

LEE *doesn't move.*

Lee.

BETH *throws her Biro across the desk to him.*

Write it down.

LEE *writes.*

Thank you.

Okay, quickly, we're going to go through this in bullet-point format, easy to remember, now what two deductions did Charles Darwin make from his observations of population numbers…? All together now…

ALL. Most offspring don't survive…

BETH. And thus!

ALL. All organisms must have to struggle for survival.

BETH. Good! And the ones that do survive will…?

ALL. Pass on their genes.

BETH. Fantastic, we are concentrating today, people. What we have just described is 'survival of the fittest'. Organisms with *less survival value* (write it down, please) will most likely die first, leaving the strongest and the fittest to pass on their genes. Please remember that 'strongest and fittest' does not necessarily mean physically strong and physically fit, it means the individual best-suited to the environment. We call this *adaptation* (write it down, please). A good example of this is the cockroach.

BETH *uploads a slide of the cockroach.*

LEAH. Gross, Miss!

BETH. Yes, but a very good example all the same. Over the centuries, as cockroaches have shared accommodation with man, they have become smaller and flatter over time to *adapt* to a domestic environment. So each generation of cockroaches has had easier access to your larders and to places to hide from you.

LEAH. Rank.

DAVEY. That's rough, Miss.

BETH. Do you see how by 'strongest and fittest', I mean best-adapted? You would assume that the biggest and bulkiest cockroaches would survive, but not if it makes them easier to squash –

LEAH*'s phone beeps.*

LEAH *checks her phone.*

(*To* LEAH.) Pass it over, please.

LEAH. Hang on a minute, Miss.

BETH. Give me the phone, Leah.

LEAH. Oh my gosh…

DANIELLE. What is it?

BETH. Leah.

LEAH. Oh my gosh, no… !

DANIELLE. What is it, Leah?

LEAH. It's Tamara.

LEAH *starts to pack her bag.*

BETH. Leah? Leah, what do you think you're doing?

LEAH. I've gotta go, Miss. It's Tamara.

BETH. I don't care who it is, you're not leaving my classroom.

DANIELLE. What's wrong?

BETH. It's her boyfriend, Miss.

DANIELLE. What is it?

LEAH. It's Ethan. Ethan Daniels. You know, in 12B?

BETH. Yes, I know.

LEAH. He's dead, Miss.

He's dead.

Beat.

She's, like, my best friend.

DANIELLE. I'm your best friend.

LEAH. Shut up, Danielle. Her boyfriend's dead. Is your boyfriend dead?

DANIELLE. He's not my –

LEAH. No. So shut up.

DAVEY. Don't tell her to shut up!

LEAH. Ah, fuck's sake. Get a room.

Can I go, Miss?

Beat.

Miss?

BETH. Yes. All right, you can go.

LEAH *stands up.*

LEE. Miss, I know a dead guy, can I go?

LEAH. Lee!

LEE. Well, I do. Darren Cassock, Miss? He lives on my estate. Only three floors down. I know his mum could use a visit, can I go?

DAVEY. Can I go, Miss?

BETH. No –

DAVEY. Mikey Bassett and Mark Reed live on my estate, Miss. Mark Reed shot through the face, Miss.

BETH. Davey.

DAVEY. It was all over the news.

BETH. No. None of you can go. Sit down, Leah.

LEAH. What?

BETH. I said sit down.

LEAH. But, Miss!

BETH. Leah. Sit. Down.

LEAH *sits*.

None of you are leaving. We are going to finish this revision session.

Uproar.

(*Over the uproar.*) Your exams are in four weeks. Four. Weeks. (*To the boys.*) You are lucky, neither of you boys has been called yet, so you can stay here and you can study. You can study for your future. And before you know it you're going to be sitting in that exam room and you'll need answers. You'll need C-grade answers. Otherwise you're not going on to college. You're not going anywhere.

That's enough!

LEAH. But, Miss, he's dead.

BETH. Everybody in this room knows somebody who is dead!

LEAH. Do you know somebody who is dead?

BETH. Yes! Of course I do!

LEAH. But not your boyfriend, Miss –

BETH. No. Nobody's boyfriend is dead.

LEAH. Tamara's is –

BETH. Nobody in this room's boyfriend is dead. Nobody in this room's boyfriend has even been called. And until that time we will stay in here and finish our revision session!

Pause while they all register what has just been said.

MMOMA. I don't have a boyfriend, Miss. Can I go?

The light narrows on BETH.

BETH *sinks into her chair.*

She takes off her comfortable shoes and puts on her high heels.

She takes out her make-up bag and applies some lip gloss.

She takes out a bottle and sprays herself with perfume.

The light extends to MMOMA.

BETH. Mmoma.

MMOMA. Umm, smells nice, Miss.

Beat.

Sorry, Miss. I'm always forgetting my books.

BETH. That's all right.

Beat.

You know, you're the only one who bothers to take them home.

MMOMA. Well…

BETH. You'll do well, Mmoma.

MMOMA. You think?

BETH. Yes. I do. You're intelligent. You have an inquisitive mind. You could be a scientist. You could.

MMOMA. Oh… thanks.

MMOMA *gets her books and moves to the door.*

Miss?

BETH. Yes?

MMOMA. Your boyfriend, Miss.

BETH. My fiancé.

MMOMA. Sorry, Miss, your fiancé.

BETH. What about him?

MMOMA. Will he go?

BETH. I don't know. He's not been called yet.

MMOMA. But will he sign up, though?

BETH. I don't know. I don't know.

MMOMA. You be proud of him, if he does. Right?

Like they said in assembly: 'Luke, team captain, off to join the greatest team of all.' Signed up. Gone.

BETH. Brave boy.

MMOMA. Yeah.

I couldn't do that, sign up, Miss. I'd die. I would. I'd point my gun and they'd knock it out my hand and I'd die. I couldn't do it. I've not got what it takes. It's lucky they don't call us, Miss. If they forced me I'd run. I run away to… where's a place where you can be safe… prison. Yeah, what was that thing… what was it? It was the Chinese, or something… they said it was like the best military tactic ever! Where, on the front line, the warriors on the front line, when they met the other side on the battlefield, they killed themselves! Stuck their swords into their stomachs to show that they were fearless. But they were prisoners. Those men, on the front line, they were on death row back home. They were going to die anyway. They were just doing what was going be done.

I'd have to be on death row. I'd have to be facing the electric chair before I would go somewhere else to die. Does that make me a coward? Miss, does it make me a coward cos I want to live?

Sorry, Miss.

But you know. You know how you were saying that 'survival of the fittest' isn't actually meaning the fittest or strongest, right?

BETH. Yes.

MMOMA. Well, it's like the cockroaches, isn't it, this war? It's the biggest and the strongest that's going to get squashed. And like, me, and you, with your chest, and like, Martin in 12C, he gets ear infections, so he can't go; it's going to be us that's best-adapted, right? Cos, we're not going. So, we're the ones who survive. We're the fittest.

Pause.

You doing something nice tonight, Miss?

BETH. I'm going out to dinner.

MMOMA. With your fiancé?

BETH. Yes.

MMOMA. He taking you out?

BETH. Yes.

MMOMA. That's nice. He looks after you, does he? Takes care of you?

Beat.

That's nice, Miss.

Have a nice time.

BETH. Thanks. You have a good weekend too.

MMOMA. Yeah, Bye.

The light narrows on MMOMA *as she looks back on* BETH.

The light closes on MMOMA.

The light opens on DANIELLE *and* DAVEY.

DANIELLE *has laid out a picnic of sandwiches, chocolates, crisps and drinks.*

DAVEY. Danielle, this is amazing.

DANIELLE. It's nothing.

DAVEY. Amazing.

DANIELLE. No. Yeah?

DAVEY. Yeah, look at this… all of this. Oh my God… (*Picks up a chocolate bar.*) You can't even get these any more!

DANIELLE. Yeah I know.

DAVEY. Where did you get this? I haven't seen one of these in, like, months.

DANIELLE. Have it.

DAVEY. Where d'you get it?

DANIELLE. My stepdad, he, like, does this.

DAVEY. What?

DANIELLE. Hoards stuff. In the cellar. He's got, like, a whole… bunker full of stuff. You know, in case –

DAVEY. No way, that's amazing. You mean, like, he's got this stuff, stuff like this, all underground?

DANIELLE. Yeah.

DAVEY. I heard about people that do that, my mum never. She would never, she's always going on about there being no need, you know, cos we're going to win. She's always saying that. And my dad, well, he's old now, but he's always saying if he were young and strong and fearless… but that's amazing for you that they… don't.

Beat.

(*Picking up a packet of sweets.*) Ah, I forget what these taste like. This is amazing.

DAVEY*'s eyes bulge as he reaches for a sandwich.*

DANIELLE *sits in silence.*

This is so good. I'm so hungry.

DANIELLE. What are those?

DANIELLE *points at the papers on top of* DAVEY*'s books.*

DAVEY. What? Oh.

Just forms.

DANIELLE. What are they?

DAVEY. Just forms, Danielle. Give us another sandwich.

DANIELLE *reaches for the forms, they are recruitment documents from the army.*

DANIELLE. Davey, what are you doing with these?

DAVEY. My dad took me to the recruitment centre.

DANIELLE. Why were you going there, you haven't been called?

DAVEY. My dad, he's been going on at me for ages and I thought if I'd just hear them out, then maybe –

DANIELLE. Davey!

DAVEY. – they'd leave me alone.

Beat.

My dad, he's doing most of the talking… talking about 'This Great War.' 'This Just War.' How he would be proud –

DANIELLE. He proud when you were fighting in the playground? Did he not pull you off one another and scold you for scrapping like a pair of dogs?

DAVEY. My dad, he's old now –

DANIELLE. You said. Fighting was for dogs.

DAVEY. But he says if he were young. And strong. And fearless.

DANIELLE. What's a dog to fear but death?

DAVEY. I'm no coward, Danielle.

DANIELLE. No. You're brave. The bravest. For saying you're more.

DAVEY. I'm right.

DANIELLE. More than dogs.

DAVEY. Right build.

DANIELLE. Master of dogs.

DAVEY. Right attitude. I should help. Protect. My family.

Beat.

I signed up.

Pause.

DANIELLE. What about your exams? What about college? What about your chance for success?

DAVEY. I'm not going to pass these exams. I can see. I can see –

DANIELLE. What?

DAVEY. – where Lee's coming from.

DANIELLE. You are nothing like Lee!

DAVEY *collects his stuff together to go.*

No. Wait.

DAVEY *stands.*

Davey!

DANIELLE *moves to him and kisses him. She wraps herself around him and kisses him passionately. She tries to undress him. He stops her and gently pushes her off.*

DAVEY. Danielle, wait.

Not now.

DANIELLE. Why not?

DAVEY. Let's make it last. I want to keep…

Let me look at you.

You're beautiful.

Go.

DANIELLE. No.

DAVEY. Go home.

DANIELLE. I don't want to go home.

DAVEY. Go home before…

DANIELLE *backs away from him, disappointed and distressed.*

DAVEY *picks himself up. Adjusts his groin. Winces.*

The lights extends to MMOMA.

MMOMA. Hi, Davey.

DAVEY. All right.

MMOMA. I forgot my books.

DAVEY. Right.

DAVEY *gets his things together.*

MMOMA. You all right?

You're walking funny.

DAVEY. Yeah. Right. No, I'm good. Thanks.

See ya then.

MMOMA. Davey?

DAVEY. Yeah?

MMOMA. I got some chocolate, d'you want some?

DAVEY. No thanks. I'm all right.

He turns away.

MMOMA. It's milk chocolate.

Sure you don't want a square?

There's not going to be much about soon.

Beat.

DAVEY. Yeah, all right, just one.

MMOMA *breaks him off a square. She has one too. They suck their chocolate.* MMOMA *grins.*

MMOMA. It's bubbly.

DAVEY. Yeah.

He wipes his mouth.

MMOMA. You got some.

DAVEY. What?

She points.

MMOMA. You got some there.

DAVEY *wipes the wrong side of his face.* MMOMA *laughs.*

No, you idiot. Here.

She gets up close, wipes his face.

They look at each other. She moves in to kiss him.

DAVEY. Woah. No. Mmoma, no.

MMOMA. What?

DAVEY *backs off.*

DAVEY. I'm with Danielle, Mmoma.

MMOMA. But –

DAVEY. Me and Danielle. We're together.

MMOMA. But you –

DAVEY. But nothing, Mmoma. You've got to stop this.

MMOMA. What?

DAVEY. Stop it, Mmoma, it's not on. It's not fair.

MMOMA. I never –

DAVEY. I'm trying, Mmoma… I'm waiting on a piece of
    heaven with Danielle. So stay away from me, Mmoma,
    please. You've got to find your own boyfriend.

MMOMA. Where am I going to get a boyfriend from? There's,
    like, three girls to every one boy left in this school.

DAVEY. That's not my problem, Mmoma. Just stay away from
    me, all right? Please, I don't want to do anything to… any-
    thing to… Just stay away from me, please.

The light narrows.

The light closes on DAVEY *and* MMOMA, *and opens on* LEAH *and* DANIELLE.

LEAH *wails,* DANIELLE *rocks her.*

DANIELLE. It's all right. It's going to be all right…

LEAH. Lee…

The light extends to LEE.

He takes her in his arms.

The light extends to the rest of the class.

BETH. What is it? What's happened? What is it now, Leah?

DANIELLE. You shouldn't be angry, Miss.

BETH. I'm not angry. Tell me what's happened.

DANIELLE. It's her brother.

BETH. He's dead.

DANIELLE. He's missing.

BETH. Oh thank God.

LEAH. So? Missing is dead. Dead is missing. It's the same thing.

BETH. I'm sorry, Leah. I'm so sorry. You don't have to be here. You should go home.

LEAH. I don't want to go home.

BETH. Go home and be with your mum, Leah.

LEAH. I don't want to be with my mum. She's just crying and crying. She says she doesn't want me around. She just wants her boy. Just wants her boy back. 'I want my boy! My beautiful boy! That's all I want! Just give me my boy back and I won't ask for anything ever again!'

I don't want to go home, Miss. Please, don't make me go home.

Beat.

BETH. All right, Leah. But can you concentrate? Can you work?

LEAH. Yes! Yes, Miss. I can work.

BETH. Can you stop crying?

LEAH *wipes her face*.

LEAH. Yes, Miss. Yes.

BETH. Then let's work.

Everybody sit down.

LEE *lets go of* LEAH.

LEAH. Lee…

BETH. It's all right. You can sit together.

LEAH. What…?

BETH. You can sit together.

DANIELLE. What about us?

BETH. You can sit together too.

LEE *and* LEAH *sit together,* DANIELLE *and* DAVEY *sit together, and* MMOMA *sits alone*.

Okay. We've got a lot to get through today. I want to tie up evolution, so let's talk about 'Genetic Variation'. Nobody can do any work if they don't have a pen or paper…

Everyone immediately gets out pens and paper, DAVEY *pulls his jumper off over his head*.

Okay. Thank you. What do we know about genetic variation, everybody together, please?

ALL. Genetic variation is the raw material of evolution.

BETH. Without genetic variation a population cannot evolve in response to a changing environment and as a result can face an increased risk of extinction.

What can cause a sudden loss in genetic variation, Mmoma?

MMOMA. Inbreeding.

BETH. Yes. What else, Danielle?

DANIELLE. Reduced population numbers...?

BETH. What can reduce population numbers?

MMOMA. Migration?

BETH. Migration, yes. What else, Davey?

Davey?

LEE. War.

Beat.

BETH. War. Yes. Earthquake. Typhoon. Natural disasters.

Nobody is writing this down. Write it down.

They all struggle to write it down.

Examples in nature of populations with low genetic variation include the cheetah and the basking shark. Both populations are at great risk of being wiped out by disease or sudden change to the environment. If the genetic make-up of a population is so unvaried that no genes can be found to have resistance to disease or that can adapt to a changing environment then...

LEE *gets up.*

Lee?

Lee, sit down, please.

LEAH. What is it, Lee?

LEE *is at the window, looking out.*

LEAH *gets up and goes to the window.*

BETH. Leah. Sit down. Leah –

DANIELLE. What is it?

LEE. Trucks. What are those trucks for, Miss? They're backing onto the playing field.

The others get up.

BETH. Sit down, everyone. Mmoma. Davey... Danielle, sit down.

They all go to the window.

DANIELLE. There's masses of them, Miss. Come and look. There's, like, five lorries backing onto the pitch.

BETH. All of you, sit down!

DAVEY. They're ruining the pitch, Miss.

BETH. Sit down.

DANIELLE. But look, Miss!

BETH. I know.

DANIELLE. What?

BETH. I know about the trucks. Please sit down.

LEAH. They're unloading. Boxes, Miss. Look at that. Loads of boxes. What's in the boxes, Miss?

DAVEY. Food?

BETH. No, not food, Davey.

LEAH. What is it, Miss?

DANIELLE. Yeah, what is it?

DAVEY. If it's not food, then what is it, Miss?

BETH. Uniforms.

DAVEY. What?

DANIELLE. What?

BETH. Uniforms. The boxes are full of uniforms.

DANIELLE. School uniforms?

BETH. No, Danielle. Not school uniforms.

They all speak at once.

LEE. Army uniforms?

LEAH. Why are they bringing army uniforms here?

DAVEY. You get your uniform at your barracks, Miss.

DANIELLE (*to* DAVEY). How d'you know that?

LEAH. Is that true, Miss? Is it army uniforms?

DANIELLE (*to* DAVEY). Know that already, do you?

BETH. If you all stop speaking at the same time then I can tell you!

They fall silent.

Yes, they are army-issue uniforms.

Uproar.

Be quiet! They are here because our school has been put forward by the headmistress to help with the war effort.

LEAH. What's that mean?

DANIELLE. Why? Why would we help, Miss?

BETH. Because, Danielle. Because. This is a good war. A just war. Because the headmistress wants to show her support.

After-school hours, including this hour that we spend together, is going to be dedicated to helping to recycle uniforms.

LEAH. What?

DANIELLE. 'Recycle'?

LEE. What do you mean 'recycle', Miss?

BETH. I mean cleaning and pressing uniforms.

MMOMA. Used uniforms?

BETH. Yes, Mmoma. Used uniforms.

Pause.

DANIELLE. Can anyone do it? I mean, can we stay for as long as we like? We don't have to go home? If we stay and help, we won't have to go home?

BETH. Yes, if you want to stay longer than this hour, yes, you can stay as long as you like.

DANIELLE. Every day?

BETH. Yes.

DANIELLE. After school? I can stay here? I don't have to go home?

BETH. Yes, Danielle.

LEE. Fuck that.

BETH. Excuse me.

LEE. I'm not washing no used uniforms.

BETH. You don't have a choice, Lee. That's what we will be doing from now on in this detention class.

MMOMA. What about our work, Miss?

BETH. We will try to do both, won't we, Mmoma?

MMOMA. But our exams, Miss. What about our exams? They're in two weeks.

BETH. You're going to have to revise in your own time, Mmoma.

MMOMA. But, Miss, you said –

BETH. I'm afraid that's the way it is, Mmoma. I don't have a choice either.

LEE *is packing his bag.*

Lee?

LEE. I'm not doing this.

BETH. I'm sorry?

LEE. Be sorry all you want, I said I'm not washing no used uniforms.

BETH. Oh right. Too much of a man? Is that it?

LEE. Whatever.

LEE *picks up his bag and makes to go.*

Lee, sit down! You are not leaving my classroom!

LEE *ignores her.*

You are not leaving my classroom. You will sit down and you will revise for your exam –

LEE. What's the point!

BETH. Lee –

LEE. What's the fucking point?

He laughs.

You're crazy.

BETH. Excuse me?

LEE. You got dead men's uniforms piling up on the playing field and you want us to sit in here and revise the hormones of your menstrual cycle.

Short pause.

BETH. Yes.

LEE laughs.

If you can make reference to comparative sexuality in your exam, or pinpoint the dangers of a loss in genetic variation –

LEE laughs again and shakes his head incredulously.

– then you are on course for a C-grade answer. I am trying to help you to shape your answers so that you might get a C –

LEE picks up his bag.

– because. One day this war will be over, the fighting will be over, and you will need that C. You will need a C. I am trying to give you knowledge.

LEE. Why?

BETH. So you can go to college. So you can get a higher education. So you can have success –

LEE. 'Success'? You mean so I can be a teacher, like you? So I can ride my bicycle back to the good side of town where I might find a rich man to marry me?

Beat.

Success, Miss. Do you really feel successful?

The light narrows on BETH *and* DANIELLE.

BETH. Danielle?

DANIELLE, *who was about to leave, turns to face* BETH.

DANIELLE. Yes, Miss.

BETH. Is everything all right, Danielle?

DANIELLE. Sure, Miss. What d'you mean?

BETH. Is everything all right at home?

Beat.

Danielle?

DANIELLE. Sure, of course, Miss. Why wouldn't it be? I'm fine.

BETH. It just seems that you don't want to go home.

Beat.

Danielle?

DANIELLE. I do. I want to go home.

BETH. You can tell me if something's the matter.

DANIELLE. Nothing's the matter, Miss.

The lights narrow on DANIELLE.

Everything's fine. Everything's fine.

The light extends from DANIELLE *to* DAVEY.

While DANIELLE *and* DAVEY *speak, the others load the boxes of uniforms onto the stage.*

I'm coming with you.

DAVEY. What?

DANIELLE. Take me with you.

DAVEY. You can't come with me. Shut up, Danielle.

DANIELLE. Luke went with his brother.

DAVEY. You're not my brother, Danielle.

DANIELLE. But I could come.

DAVEY. No. You can't come.

DANIELLE. Please let me come, don't leave me here.

DAVEY. Danielle, you can't come.

DANIELLE. Why not?

DAVEY. Why not? You couldn't kill anyone.

DANIELLE. You don't know.

DAVEY. Yes I do, look at you. You can't come.

DANIELLE. What's wrong with me?

DAVEY. Nothing. There's nothing wrong with you, you are what you are: a girl. And if you weren't so beautiful, if you weren't so distracting... But you can't come looking like you do.

DANIELLE. Why!

DAVEY. Because there'd be you, looking like you do, and us looking at you and... (*He imitates the sound of an explosion.*)

DAVEY *goes.*

The light narrows on DANIELLE.

She casts about, making small sounds of distress. She breathes shallowly and erratically, building herself into a frenzy.

The light extends to LEE *who has been watching her.*

Their eyes meet, and LEE *goes for her. He pushes her to the ground, pulling at her clothes. She struggles against him, kicking and scratching but he is too strong for her. He holds her down and in a moment of consent they kiss.*

The light extends to BETH.

BETH. Lee!

Lee, get off her!

BETH *manages to pull him off her, but* LEE *swings round and knocks her into a table. It crushes the wind out of her.* DANIELLE *scrabbles up and goes to her.*

DANIELLE. Miss? Miss, are you all right!

BETH *is struggling for breath, she begins to have an asthma attack. She wheezes and panics.*

BETH. Danielle… Danielle. Get my bag… my bag.

DANIELLE. Where is it, Miss?

BETH. On… the… desk…

DANIELLE *turns towards the desk but* LEE *is already at the desk, holding the bag. He pulls out the inhaler.*

BETH *sucks in air.*

DANIELLE. Lee. Lee, give me the inhaler. Please.

LEE *stands watching* BETH. *She looks back at him, drawing in deep, hoarse, strangled breaths. They stare at each other.*

Lee. Lee. Please.

LEE *watches* BETH *with a mixture of menace and curiosity as she succumbs to the attack. When she looks like she is about to pass out,* LEE *comes to and shakily passes the inhaler to* DANIELLE. DANIELLE *takes the inhaler and presses it to* BETH*'s lips.*

Miss? Miss, here.

She helps her to work the inhaler, and the attack subsides. LEE *has backed into the doorway.*

The lights narrow on BETH *and* LEE *on opposite sides of the stage.*

The light closes on them.

The door slams.

DAVEY *can be heard banging on the door.*

DAVEY (*shouts*). Danielle!

Open the door!

DAVEY *bangs harder on the door.*

Danielle, open the fucking door.

The light opens on DAVEY *and* DANIELLE. *He bangs on the door from inside the classroom.* DANIELLE *has locked him in.*

DANIELLE. No, Davey, please listen to me.

DAVEY. Danielle, open this door!

DAVEY *violently rattles the door and twists the doorknob.*

LEAH *and* MMOMA *run on.*

LEAH. Danielle?

DANIELLE (*to* DAVEY). Please, Davey, think about what you're saying.

LEAH. Danielle, what are you doing?

DAVEY. I'm going to fucking kill him.

DANIELLE. Think, Davey. Please just calm down.

DAVEY. Open this fucking door! I'm going to fucking wipe the floor with him.

LEAH. No!

DANIELLE. No. You stay in there and you calm down and you think about what you're saying, please, Davey. I am asking you to be –

DAVEY *throws himself at the door.*

The girls scream.

Stop it, Davey!

DAVEY *continues to throw himself at the door, the wood splinters.*

LEAH. Stop it, Davey, you're breaking the door!

DAVEY *pounds the door.*

MMOMA *runs off.*

DANIELLE. Please, Davey. Stop it. Think about it. Please. Don't be just like him. Be more.

MMOMA *returns with* BETH.

BETH. Danielle, who's in there?

Danielle?

DANIELLE. Davey.

BETH *takes a key from her pocket and unlocks the door.*

DAVEY *comes crashing through the door, panting and heaving.*

Davey, calm down, please. Calm down and listen to me.

DAVEY *thrashes about in frustration.*

Davey, if you show me that you're listening to me then that will improve your situation right now.

DAVEY *rams the wall.*

BETH *raises her walkie-talkie to her mouth. She tries to patch in, but receives only static.*

W11C to Referral Base, receiving?

Only static is heard back. She shakes the walkie-talkie.

Hello, W11C, can you hear me?

LEE *appears in the corridor, he spins on his heel.*

Davey –

DAVEY. Lee! Get back here!

BETH. Davey, you stay where you are.

LEE *turns to run.* DAVEY *breaks past* BETH *and leaps on him. They tussle across the stage, throwing struggled punches, rolling and knocking into furniture.*

The girls back away and for a moment stare in silent curiosity. LEAH, DANIELLE *and* MMOMA *look at one another and then shriek.*

Lee... Davey... Stop.

BETH *desperately tries to patch in on her walkie-talkie.*

Karen, Karen, can you hear me? I need help!

There is only static in response.

Can you hear me! Karen!

BETH *gives up on the walkie-talkie and goes in to break them up. She gets between them both and they writhe and grope together.* BETH *ends facing* LEE, *their faces close together, breath on each other. She pushes him off her and stands between them with her arms outstretched.*

Enough. Stupid. Stupid. Boys.

The boys stay apart.

BETH *sees that her walkie-talkie has been crushed in the struggle and lies in pieces on the ground. She bends and picks up the pieces.*

What. Am I. Going to do?

LEE. Nothing.

I'm going.

BETH. What...?

LEE. I'm going. I got called. My letter came through this morning.

LEAH. What!

LEE. I'm going.

Going to join the fight. Not some dog-scrap in the classroom.

A real fight. A man's fight. The only fight that matters.

(*To the girls.*) This will be my success: I am going to fight for you.

DAVEY. You're a cowardly bastard, that's what you are.

LEE. I am going to be a soldier.

(*Points to his chest.*) A soldier.

A soldier's got to have a uniform.

I need me a uniform –

LEE *goes to the boxes.*

BETH. Lee, don't –

LEE. Soldier's got to have a uniform…

BETH. They're not ready, Lee.

LEE *takes hold of a box.*

LEE. Can't fight without armour…

BETH. You're not ready, Lee.

Lee, don't –

LEE *tears open a box and the bloodied, torn uniforms of dead soldiers spill out onto the floor.*

Long pause as they all look in horror.

LEE *goes.*

They continue to look in horror.

Right. Well.

Let's get started then, shall we?

Nobody moves.

They've been boxed in no particular order, from the looks of it they've just been… stuffed in, so I'd say the best way to do this is to start by sorting them into piles and once they are clean we can sort into regiment. Leah, Danielle, if you make a start on these.

Everyone appears to be in a slight daze.

Danielle? Leah?

DANIELLE *and* LEAH *move to the boxes and begin to slowly unpack.*

Throughout the following exchange, LEAH *quietly searches through the name tags on the uniforms, looking for her brother's.*

So all trousers over here, boots down there for polishing – Mmoma, will you take the boots?

MMOMA *walks to a box and pulls out a boot.*

That's it. Good girl.

MMOMA *looks to* BETH.

We need two boots per... person, don't we? Each person has two feet.

MMOMA *turns back to the box and pulls out another boot.*

Right. Right and left. Each person needs one right boot and one left boot.

MMOMA *looks at the boots.*

We'll sort it out later. Just bring them down here.

Okay, jackets on the line and buttons... collect up any loose buttons you find, if they're hanging on by a thread they'll need re-sewing, so pull them off and keep them together.

DANIELLE *holds up a jacket that has been shot through the middle and is torn to pieces.*

BETH *looks at the jacket.*

And we best start a pile for items that obviously cannot be recycled.

Beat.

Okay! Brushes are here, stiff-bristle brushes first, let's get the mud and dried... off first. Davey –

DAVEY *goes.*

And then they can go in to soak, with the stain remover.
Where's the stain remover? Danielle, will you –

DANIELLE *follows* DAVEY.

Danielle?

I'll come back with the stain remover.

You just carry on putting things in piles, girls, okay? Okay.

BETH *looks at* LEAH, *who is quietly checking the name tags.*

BETH *is horrified. She goes.*

MMOMA *unpacks in silence.*

LEAH *checks the name tags.*

MMOMA *picks up a bloodied helmet, she holds it away from her and turns it upside down. Nothing falls out. She continues to hold it at arm's length.*

Suddenly MMOMA *puts the helmet on her head.*

LEAH *looks at her.* MMOMA *stands still.*

LEAH *puts on a helmet.*

They both stand still.

Suddenly they race to dress in full army-issue uniform.

They fall into mock combat, sloping around the room ducking under desks, evading a shared enemy. They shout commands to each other, popping up from under cover of tables and chairs.

MMOMA *assumes the name Dwayne.* LEAH *assumes the name Chuck. They speak with a deep American drawl.*

'Dwayne' (MMOMA) *is hit, he falls to the ground.*

MMOMA. Chuck! Chuck, where are you?

Chuck (LEAH) *rushes to his side.*

LEAH. I'm here, Dwayne. I'm here, right by your side.

MMOMA. Chuck!

LEAH. Dwayne!

MMOMA. Chuck, listen to me.

LEAH. I'm listening to you.

MMOMA. I need you to do something for me.

LEAH. What, Dwayne? Anything, anything you want...

MMOMA. I need you to give a message to my mother.

LEAH. No, Dwayne! Don't talk like that. Don't talk like that, Dwayne.

MMOMA. Listen to me. Listen to me! I need you to tell my mother. I need you to tell her I loved her and I only tried to make her proud.

LEAH. Dwayne –

MMOMA. And Cecelia. My love. My beautiful –

LEAH. Beautiful!

MMOMA. – Cecelia. I need you to give her something from me.

LEAH. What, Dwayne? Anything, Dwayne.

MMOMA. I want you to give her these chest hairs –

MMOMA *pretends to pluck some chest hairs.*

– for the locket round her neck. Promise me, Chuck. Promise me.

LEAH. I promise you, Dwayne. I'll give 'em to her. I swear it.

MMOMA. You take care of her –

LEAH. I will –

MMOMA. You look out for my beautiful –

LEAH. Beautiful!

MMOMA. – Cecelia. But don't you touch her.

LEAH. What?

MMOMA. Don't you lay a finger on my beautiful Cecilia, all right?

LEAH. Come on now, Chuck.

MMOMA. You listen to me, friend, you touch my Ceclia in her special place and I swear this brother's gonna come back from the grave to haunt your ass, you hear me? You hear me!

LEAH. I hear you. I hear you, Dwayne. Loud and clear.

MMOMA. It's getting cold, Chuck. It's getting real cold.

LEAH. No, Dwayne. Stay with me, Dwayne.

MMOMA. It's so cold. It's so cold.

LEAH. No, Dwayne, come on, Dwayne –

BETH enters unnoticed and watches in horror.

MMOMA. And the light. I can see a light, Chuck.

LEAH. No! Dwayne! Stay away from the light.

MMOMA. It's beautiful…

LEAH. Dwayne –

MMOMA. Even more beautiful than Cecelia.

LEAH. Dwayne, you listen to me. Whatever you do, Dwayne, stay away from the light!

Dwayne dies.

Dwayne! No!

LEAH *pulls* MMOMA *into her chest.*

Dwayne!

LEAH *sees* BETH. *She drops* MMOMA. *She stares at her in horror.*

The girls stand up and look down at their uniforms.

Suddenly and desperately they try to undress.

BETH. Girls. Girls. It's all right. Calm down.

They claw at themselves, tearing and pulling, throwing the clothes to the floor.

Leah –

Mmoma –

Stop it –

MMOMA *throws down the last of her uniform and backs into a corner.*

Mmoma –

LEAH *is still trying desperately to pull her jacket off over her head, but it gets stuck around her neck and she tries to yank it off, strangling herself. She yanks and yanks and starts to choke.*

Leah. Leah, calm down –

BETH *tries to help her.*

Leah, calm down, I can't help you if you don't calm down!

BETH *grabs the jacket and pulls it off her head.* LEAH *snatches it and desperately inspects the name tag.*

The light narrows on LEAH.

LEAH. Jonathan. Jonathan Mayr.

The light closes on LEAH.

The light opens on MMOMA.

MMOMA *takes a uniform jacket and hangs it on the line. She shakes out a damp pair of army-issue trousers. She is about to hang them up when she holds them in line under the jacket. She pegs the trousers to the jacket. She slips the ends of the trousers into a pair of boots. She gets on a chair to hang a helmet from a hook. She steps back and looks at the soldier.*

She smiles coyly. She looks at him out of the corner of her eye. She giggles and turns away.

MMOMA. What?

She turns back.

My name?

Oh. Um. Mmoma.

Mmoma.

Oh, thank you. Yes, it is exotic. Nigerian. Africa.

The great wide Africa.

No, I never been. But. I'm going to. Going to go to Nigeria, Africa. Step off the plane and be like, 'I'm home…'

What was that? Oh, you think so? You're sweet.

What my, my eyes? Yes, they are big.

She touches her hair.

Oh, thank you. I had it done.

She looks down at her body.

Oh don't, you'll make me blush. Well, I do try to keep myself in shape. I don't eat all junk and –

She covers her behind, shocked.

'Scuse me, I don't think you should even be looking there.

Shame on you. What are you like?

Tut. Tut. Tut.

She turns away and surreptitiously shows him her bottom.

Sorry, what was that?

She turns back.

No. I'm still at school.

Why, did you think I was older?

I get that a lot.

I never get ID'd, never, not even at Price Smart on the High Street, and they're, like, well strict –

What, sorry?

You what? You want to know everything?

Everything there is to know? About me?

Well. My gosh. Where to start...?

What do I wanna be? When I grow up?

I'm actually quite grown up already.

But, when I leave school? Well. My mum wants me to be a doctor. Everyone wants me to try and get to be a doctor or a pharmacist or... But. Really. Deep, right deep down, in me. Is a singer!

That's right. I'm gonna be a musician!

My inspiration?

Shirley. Shirley Bassey: the most greatest singer that ever was!

The most beautiful strong black British daughter-of-a-Nigerian singing woman – that is gonna be me!

Of course I can sing!

Show you?

All right then. Take a seat. Okay, you can stand.

MMOMA *clears her throat.*

Ready?

MMOMA *sings the first few lines of Shirley Bassey's '(Where Do I Begin) Love Story', impersonating the singer.*

There you go.

Thank you! I do sound like her, don't I?

I can feel it, you know? In my belly. It's not about brains, is it? It's about gut. It comes from the gut and boils up. You lose your head.

You lose your head.

There is a noise.

MMOMA *starts, she turns to leave. Stops.*

Tomorrow?

I don't know… I think I'm busy.

Day after?

I think I might be busy then too.

What? Here?

You'll be here waiting?

Every day?

Well.

I'll think about it.

The light narrows on MMOMA *as she walks away, wiggling her behind.*

The light closes on MMOMA *and opens on* LEE. *He is dressed as a soldier. He carries a bag on his back.*

The light extends to LEAH; *she sees him and gasps.*

LEAH. Shit, Lee, I didn't even recognise you. Look. Look at you.

You's dressed like a soldier.

LEE. I am a soldier.

LEAH. Not yet.

LEE. Fourteen days. Fourteen days' training. Then I'm a soldier.

Beat.

LEAH. Shit, Lee.

LEE. Yeah.

Yeah.

LEE *adjusts his bag.*

So. Well. I'll see ya.

LEAH. Yeah.

I'll see ya.

LEE. Yeah.

LEE *turns. Then stops.*

Leah?

LEAH. Yes, Lee?

LEE. Don't you think it's funny that our names are, like, Leah and Lee? Like, sound the same? If you say them together really fast. Leah and Leah, Leah and Lee, Leah and Lee. Say it.

LEE *(together)*. Leah and Lee Leah and Lee Leah and Lee…

LEAH *(together)*. Leah and Lee Leah and Lee Leah and Lee…

LEE. You can't tell which is which.

LEAH *(laughs)*. Yeah. No. Can't.

Beat.

LEE. We never talked about that before.

LEAH. No. We never.

LEE. You would have thought we would, though.

LEAH. I guess.

LEE. Have talked about it.

But it was always, like, 'Leah and Lee'. You know? That's the way it always was.

LEAH. Yeah.

LEE. Yeah.

Pause.

So, yeah. See ya.

He turns to go.

LEAH. Lee.

Lee!

He stops.

LEE. What?

LEAH. You let off a bomb, Lee. You can't just let off a bomb and walk out without a scratch. You can't just leave me to pick up the pieces of, of, of what you destroy, Lee. What am I supposed to do? You're supposed to be my boyfriend.

You were supposed to be my boyfriend.

I had a boyfriend.

LEE. I'm sorry, Leah.

LEAH. That's not enough, Lee. That's just not enough!

LEE. I can't explain it.

LEAH. Explain it!

LEE. It's, like… it's –

LEAH. What?

LEE. It's like –

LEAH. What!

LEE. – the way it is! It's the way it is, Leah!

LEAH. No.

LEE. You get these. Feelings.

LEAH. What feelings?

LEE. Feelings. Urges. The blood moves.

LEAH. You're full of shit.

LEE. It's not just me, Leah. You don't hear them. You don't hear us in them changing rooms. You don't know the things we say. The things we think. And when the cleaning lady came in one day when we was all charged and sweating and we were looking at her like a pack of dogs. We could have gone for her like a pack of dogs.

I had to hold onto the bench.

Beat.

LEAH. You're sick.

LEE. I can't control it. I can't get on top of it. Sometimes it gets on top of me. Maybe it's a good thing, Leah, that I'm going.

LEAH. No.

LEE. Maybe it is. I'm not doing any good here. I'm not doing any good. Maybe I can do good for here, if I'm not here any more.

Pause.

LEAH *looks at the ground.*

After a moment, LEE *drops his head also.*

The light extends to BETH.

BETH. Lee?

LEE *looks up.*

Lee, your mum is downstairs in reception.

LEE *nods.*

The light narrows to LEAH *and* LEE.

LEE. I gotta go.

LEAH *stares at the floor.*

Leah…

LEE *turns.*

LEAH. What if you die? What if, when you get there, you die?

LEE. I'm not going to die.

LEAH. No? Not when they're shooting at you? Not when they're blowing you up? Or tying you up and beating you? Treating you like… an animal. Wishing you would die.

LEE. Leah.

LEAH. What when you do?

LEE. If I do, you going be happy those were the last words you said to me?

LEAH. I love you. I don't know why, but I do.

Short pause.

LEE. I love you.

LEAH. Do you? Really?

LEE. You're my girlfriend.

LEAH smiles.

The light extends to BETH, MMOMA *and* DANIELLE.

BETH. Lee. Your mum's waiting.

LEE nods, pulls on his bag and stands proud and tall.

The women stand before him.

Good luck, Lee.

This is a great war.

This is a just war.

Come home proud, Lee.

MMOMA. Come home glorious.

DANIELLE. Come home victorious.

LEAH. Come home.

Come home.

The light narrows and closes on the women.

When the light opens they are sorting through the uniforms.

They talk as they work.

BETH. When a new colony is established by a small number of individuals, the loss of genetic variation may lead to this daughter population being genetically very different from the parent population. In extreme cases this can lead to the evolution of a new species.

What do we call this, Danielle?

DANIELLE. I can't remember…

BETH. Try, Danielle.

DANIELLE. I can't remember, Miss.

BETH. Mmoma, can you remember?

MMOMA. The Founder Effect, Miss.

BETH. The Founder Effect, yes.

The smaller the size of the daughter population, the less likely their genetic make-up will represent that of the parent population. In short this means that the new population may be very different…

BETH *takes a breath*.

The Founder Effect –

MMOMA. Miss?

BETH. Yes.

MMOMA. What was is it, Miss? I came. I saw…

BETH. I conquered.

MMOMA. Yeah. This. This is a weak man's war, isn't it, Miss? There's only one winner. And the weak man will be king. Did you know, Miss, Martin in 12C, he's the one with the cracked face and the ear infections so bad that he's got to lie with his head on the ground? Well now, Sue-Ellen lies with him. Sue-Ellen, Miss. Sue-Ellen is better-looking than Danielle and she's lying on the lunch-hall floor with Martin from 12C. Martin from 12C won't look twice at me and his face falls into his food.

BETH. Mmoma.

MMOMA. This is the weak man's war, isn't it, Miss? He came. He sat at the back and saw. And now he conquers.

BETH. Mmoma.

MMOMA. He is The Founder.

Beat.

BETH. The Founder Effect was first fully outlined in 1952 by –

DANIELLE. Why can't women be called, Miss? Why aren't we in the draft?

BETH. I don't know, Danielle. In 1952 by Ernst Mayr –

DANIELLE. I don't think that's right, Miss.

BETH. Who knows how to spell Mayr?

DANIELLE. It shouldn't be only men.

LEAH. M. A. Y. R.

BETH. That's right, Leah, well done.

DANIELLE. Women should be encouraged to go.

BETH. Think about the genetics, Danielle.

DANIELLE. But, Miss –

BETH. The genetics, Danielle. In order for a population to survive you need more females than males. An entire population can be founded with one male. One seed. But one female cannot sustain growth, Danielle. More women must stay behind.

Beat.

DANIELLE *looks torn.*

Men will fight if they can, Danielle.

DANIELLE. Why!

BETH. Because they are animals.

DANIELLE. I am an animal.

BETH. And that is why you do not fight.

Men have been fighting since before they were men, Danielle. And we, we have been making more of them.

M.A.Y.R.

LEAH. From a squit?

BETH. What?

LEAH. Before they were men. They were a squit.

BETH. A squirt.

LEAH. Squirt?

BETH. Sea squirt.

LEAH. Yeah. If from a sea squirt comes a fish. And from a fish comes a monkey, and from a monkey comes me. And this – (*Points to the length of her body.*) this is the way I come. Chemicals in my blood. Chemicals from the monkey, who got them from the fish, who got them from the squirt. We all come from the squirt.

BETH. Yes.

LEAH. Then where is God?

Is God the squirt?

Beat.

BETH. No.

LEAH. Then where is God?

Beat.

Because this is today. And all my friends are dying.

I don't need a monkey, Miss. I need God.

The light narrows on BETH.

BETH *sinks into her chair.*

She takes off her comfortable shoes and puts on her high heels.

She takes out her make-up bag and applies some lip gloss.

She takes out a bottle and sprays herself with perfume.

Finally she pulls off her comfortable pants and puts on a thong.

The light extends to MMOMA, *who has been watching her.*

BETH. Mmoma.

MMOMA. Sorry, Miss. Forgot my books again.

MMOMA *gets her books.*

She stops in the doorway.

Miss?

BETH. Yes, Mmoma.

MMOMA. Do you worry, Miss?

Do you worry that if he goes, your fiancé, he won't come back?

BETH. No.

MMOMA. Can't think about it, Miss?

BETH. I wonder who will come back.

MMOMA. Yeah, Miss, I wonder too. I wonder if Luke and Aaron and Oli McGreevy… And Lee… I wonder who…

BETH. I wonder what will come back.

MMOMA. What do you mean, 'what'?

BETH. I wonder what becomes of a man when you take him outside to fight like an animal. I wonder *what* will come back.

Beat.

MMOMA. Miss –

BETH. See you tomorrow, Mmoma.

MMOMA. Miss?

BETH (*tired*). Yes.

MMOMA. Will you still do that when he's gone?

BETH. What?

MMOMA. When he's gone, will you still do that?

BETH. Do what?

MMOMA. Change your knickers.

Beat.

BETH. Excuse me?

MMOMA. I think I understand, Miss.

BETH. What did you say?

MMOMA. You taught us well, Miss.

BETH. How dare you.

MMOMA. The Founder Effect.

You're trying for a baby, Miss.

You want his baby before he goes.

BETH *stammers*.

You want to give us knowledge, Miss.

BETH. Get out.

MMOMA. And knowledge will give us success.

BETH. I said get out.

MMOMA. If success is survival, Miss.

MMOMA *points at* BETH*'s stomach*.

Then the Founder will know best.

BETH (*shouts*). Get out of my classroom.

The light narrows on MMOMA *as she runs to her soldier.*

MMOMA. You were being serious when you said you'd be
here. You've been here every day. Waiting for me.

You must like me.

You must think I'm something special.

You must see me set apart from all the other girls.

I must stand out to you in a crowd. I must make your heart
race and your tummy flutter like butterflies. Or else you

wouldn't wait here every day in the hope that I might come and talk with you.

Beat.

Bet you didn't think I actually would.

You must be pretty nervous right now.

Beat.

But it's all right, I like talking, so don't worry if your tongue gets stuck in your throat, cos I like talking and I don't really need you to answer me back. Just that you're here is enough.

I feel special.

I feel set apart from all the other girls.

I feel like I do stand out in a crowd. And that I could make your heart race and your tummy flutter like butterflies. And that's painful – butterflies are painful! (*She clutches her sternum.*) Like being on the 'Pirates of Penzance' ride when it drops. I feel like I cause you that pain. That beautiful, beautiful pain. That's why I come and talk to you. I understand your pain. I come to help you. I come to take it away.

By knowing, by having you know me.

Knowledge is the key; the fruit from the tree; knowledge is how you will love me.

MMOMA *moves to her soldier and touches his jacket. She slips one of her arms inside the arm of the jacket, bringing him to life. She slips the uniformed arm around her waist so that he is holding her. She looks up at him, and they rock slowly. His hand strays to her bottom. She stops it and pulls it back up.*

The lights narrow and close on them as they sway together.

The light opens on DANIELLE *and* DAVEY.

DANIELLE *has laid out a last supper for herself and* DAVEY. *A tablecloth covers a desk.* DANIELLE *offers* DAVEY *a sandwich.* DAVEY *turns it away.*

DANIELLE. You want something else?

DAVEY. I can't swallow.

DANIELLE. You want some water?

DAVEY. I can't swallow, Danielle.

DANIELLE. Sore throat?

DAVEY. I can't sleep.

DANIELLE. Try and eat –

She offers the sandwich again.

DAVEY. Don't you get it? I nearly walked out the house with a kitchen knife.

Beat.

My blood –

DANIELLE. Please –

DAVEY. – is boiling.

We are what we are.

DAVEY *looks at* DANIELLE *with lust.*

You are so beautiful.

DANIELLE *slowly pulls the tablecloth off the desk.*

Every time you walk and we can see you moving.

You make us crazy.

DAVEY *moves towards her.*

DANIELLE. Davey –

DAVEY. You can't deny –

DANIELLE. No.

DAVEY. – the effect you have –

DANIELLE. No, I don't deny –

DAVEY. – just by lying there –

DANIELLE. – my responsibility –

DAVEY. – for anyone to see.

DANIELLE. – to protect a man from himself.

DANIELLE pulls the tablecloth around her.

DAVEY. What are you doing?

DANIELLE. Don't look at me, please.

DAVEY. What are you doing, Danielle?

DANIELLE. I said don't look at me.

DAVEY. Uncover yourself.

DANIELLE. I am trying to help you.

DAVEY. Don't cover yourself, Danielle.

DANIELLE. Be more.

DAVEY. Not from me.

He holds up his hands to the outside world.

From them. Out there.

Don't let them get to see you.

Save yourself for me.

DAVEY *leaves.*

The light narrows on DANIELLE *and extends to* BETH.

DANIELLE. Miss?

BETH. Yes?

DANIELLE. So what you're saying, Miss, is that because of the way I have evolved. Because of the way I made it out of the caves. I have to be sexually attractive every second of every day of every year until. Until I die? Because even after menopause. That doesn't change anything, does it? You don't even get a break then. A peace. For your dying days. No. Cos they got Viagra now. Don't they? They got fucking Viagra. So it doesn't ever stop. Never. Every day.

Until you die.

Miss?

BETH. Yes.

DANIELLE. Because we survived.

BETH. Yes.

DANIELLE. I understand.

The light narrows and closes on DANIELLE *as she pulls the tablecloth tighter around her.*

The light opens on MMOMA *as she talks to her soldier.*

MMOMA. I had this doll. Shirley. For Shirley Bassey!

MMOMA *sings another few lines of Shirley Bassey's '(Where Do I Begin) Love Story'.*

I took her everywhere with me. I couldn't be without her. I used to kiss her. On the mouth. But I couldn't get my tongue in. Cos her mouth were closed. She weren't one of them dolls with the hole. But her lips were raised and slightly parted and I used to lick in the cleft. I used to sleep with her. She used to sleep with me. She were one of them dolls with the closing eyes.

I loved her. It were love. It were. But my dad took her away. Cos you're not supposed to kiss a baby on the mouth. But she weren't a baby. She were a doll. She were made of plastic. I could have put my tongue in my baby.

She were my partner. Everybody needs a partner. Doesn't matter who it is, what it is, whatever you can get; sometimes it's a dog.

It broke my heart.

It broke. My heart.

So I've got to find me a new partner. The right partner: I've got to find me a man.

So that's me. Now you know me. Know what I'm after. What I'm about. Wear my broken heart on my sleeve.

You have the knowledge. Do you love me?

The light extends to DANIELLE, *still wearing the tablecloth. She staggers, drunk.*

She carries a vodka bottle, kitchen knife, needle, thread and water.

She clears a space for herself in the middle of the room.

DANIELLE. Help me, Mmoma.

MMOMA. What are you doing?

DANIELLE. Come and help me.

MMOMA. What is this? Why are you wearing a tablecloth, Danielle?

DANIELLE. This is a knife, this is a needle, this is thread and water.

I need your help.

DANIELLE *struggles to take off her shoes.*

They do this in your country.

MMOMA. What?

DANIELLE. Where you come from.

MMOMA. I come from here, Danielle.

DANIELLE. Where you came from, before. From where you got your skin.

MMOMA. I was born here, Danielle. I've always lived here.

DANIELLE. Your mum. Where your mum's from.

They do this where she comes from, don't they?

DANIELLE *struggles to pull off her tights.*

MMOMA. Do what, Danielle?

DANIELLE *struggles with her tights.*

DANIELLE. Help me, Mmoma.

MMOMA *helps her with her tights. All the while,*
DANIELLE *keeps the tablecloth around her.*

In your mum's country they do this, don't they?

DANIELLE *pulls off her knickers.*

MMOMA. Do what, Danielle?

DANIELLE. Do this to their girls. Close them up.

MMOMA. What?

DANIELLE *opens her legs.*

DANIELLE. Cut off the lips and sew it up so there's only a
small hole, size of a matchstick.

MMOMA. Danielle!

DANIELLE. I need you to help me, Mmoma.

I need you to close me up. Sew me up so that no one can get
in there. Only a matchstick.

Beat.

MMOMA. No.

DANIELLE. They do this with the girls, so they're protected.
See?

So no one can get in there.

Not even themselves.

DANIELLE *swigs from the vodka bottle.*

MMOMA. Danielle.

DANIELLE. I've had a paracetamol.

MMOMA. Danielle, no...

DANIELLE. Come on, Mmoma. Be brave, Mmoma. You can
do it.

I would do it but I may pass out so I couldn't finish.

If I pass out you have to finish.

Promise me you'll finish, Mmoma.

MMOMA. No. Are you crazy?

DANIELLE. Please, Mmoma.

She grabs her wrist and makes her look at her.

I don't want it any more. I don't want to be open any more. Not even to myself. You have to, look –

She shows her.

Pull back the hood and cut it off.

MMOMA. No…

DANIELLE. One two three. Quick like that. It's okay. You can do it. Do it for me. Be brave, Mmoma.

She puts the knife in MMOMA*'s hands.*

Be brave.

DANIELLE *leans back.* MMOMA *looks at her vagina.*

Please, Mmoma. Help me.

Mmoma?

MMOMA *stares at her vagina.*

What is it?

MMOMA. I never seen a white one.

DANIELLE. What?

MMOMA. Well. Pink. I only ever seen mine. Mine's more brown.

DANIELLE. Is it the same shape?

MMOMA. Yeah.

DANIELLE. Really the same shape?

MMOMA. Yeah, sort of.

DANIELLE. Let me see.

MMOMA *takes off her tights and knickers and shows her.*

MMOMA. See?

DANIELLE. Yeah. Yeah, it is, those… bits… go out like that.

MMOMA. Yeah.

DANIELLE. I thought I was… weird.

MMOMA. Yeah, me too. But it's the same.

DANIELLE. Yeah.

MMOMA. We're the same.

They smile.

Show me yours again.

DANIELLE *shows her again.*

The light extends to DAVEY, *who has been watching them. He stumbles, exhausted, betrayed, defeated.*

DAVEY. Danielle…

DANIELLE *turns to see him.*

Danielle.

DANIELLE. Davey.

DAVEY. What are you…?

DANIELLE *brings her hands up to cover her groin.*

Why…?

He stumbles.

I came back for you.

His voice cracks in disappointment.

I came back for you.

DANIELLE. No.

DAVEY. Halfway there. I knew. I. Will die. And you, Danielle, were waiting…

DANIELLE. Davey –

DAVEY. And I wanted to…

DANIELLE. Davey –

DAVEY. I wanted to have you.

He cries.

DANIELLE. No.

DAVEY. I wanted to have you. And look at you… Do you know what you do to me? You couldn't do worse to me, a thousand bullets couldn't shoot me the way you. Torture me.

DANIELLE *recoils.*

DANIELLE. No. No.

DAVEY. You said you would wait for me –

DANIELLE. No I never, I said –

DAVEY. And the moment I'm gone –

DANIELLE. I said I had to protect you.

DAVEY. The *moment* I'm gone –

DANIELLE. I had to protect you from yourself.

DAVEY. You go and open yourself up to…

DAVEY *focuses on* MMOMA.

DANIELLE. Because you can't seem to stop.

DAVEY (*to* MMOMA). You.

DANIELLE. Stop.

DAVEY. You did this.

DANIELLE. Stop.

MMOMA. No, I never –

DAVEY. She's mine!

DANIELLE. Stop this!

MMOMA *takes hold of the knife, he sees*.

What's that? A knife?

You were going to cut Danielle with that? You were going to cut her with a knife?

MMOMA. No!

DANIELLE. Davey, she has nothing to do with this.

DAVEY. The moment I'm gone, you were going to cut her with a knife?

MMOMA *tries to struggle up*.

I'll cut you with a knife.

DANIELLE. No, Davey, stop this!

DAVEY *lunges for her and knocks the knife out of her hand*. DAVEY *forces* MMOMA *to the ground*.

No, Davey! Davey, stop it, please.

MMOMA *fights as hard as she can, but* DAVEY *is too strong for her.*

Please, Davey, d'you not see what you're doing?

DANIELLE *staggers in distress, still drunk*.

Eat. Fuck. Fight. Die.

Pig. Dog. Horse. Bear.

DAVEY *encircles* MMOMA*'s throat with his hands*.

Human being.

MMOMA *begins to slowly suffocate*.

Being human. Is more. Than being pig.

DANIELLE *puts her hand on her chest*.

I am more. More than mother. More than making babies. More than keeping peace: Man.

DANIELLE *grabs the knife and plunges it into* DAVEY*'s back.* DAVEY *releases his grip on* MMOMA *and sinks back into* DANIELLE*'s arms. They sit together, his back in her belly, and rock.*

DAVEY. I. I'm sorry.

DANIELLE. I'm sorry.

DAVEY. I couldn't.

DANIELLE. I know.

DAVEY. I wish I could have.

DANIELLE. I know.

DAVEY. I wish I could have been more.

DAVEY *dies.*

DANIELLE. Davey. Davey, no…

DANIELLE *recoils from him, she pulls herself away.*

What have I done?

DANIELLE *staggers across the stage and into the soldier. She looks up at the soldier. In her distress she begins to climb into the soldier's uniform.* MMOMA *approaches her, she tries to calm her.*

MMOMA. You did it.

I didn't think you would.

I thought I would die because you couldn't help me.

You did the one thing I thought you couldn't do.

Because.

DANIELLE *stands in full uniform.*

Well, look at you.

I didn't know you could be more.

They look at one another.

The light closes on them.

The light opens on BETH.

She stumbles, sucking in air.

The light extends to LEAH.

LEAH. Miss!

Miss, are you all right?

Beth –

Miss, do you need your inhaler, Miss?

Where is your inhaler?

Where is your bag? I can't find your bag. Here is your bag.
Can I go in your bag, Miss? Miss, can I go in your bag?

Shit. Go in her bag.

LEAH *goes into* BETH*'s bag and pulls out her inhaler. She
helps* BETH *to use the inhaler.*

Miss? Miss?

BETH *is crying.*

Miss, are you all right?

You were having an attack.

The light extends to MMOMA.

(*To* MMOMA.) There's something wrong with her. Maybe
she sucked too much on that thing.

MMOMA. Miss, are you all right?

BETH. Mmoma...

MMOMA. Yes, Miss.

LEAH. Get it together, Miss. We got to have a lesson, Miss.

What's wrong with her?

We've got to do these uniforms. What are we going to do
with all these uniforms...?

MMOMA. Your fiancé, he has gone now?

BETH *cries*.

Gone to join the war.

The Great War.

The Just War.

Just as he wanted.

BETH *nods through her tears*.

(*Gently.*) We have work to do, don't we? (*To* LEAH.) Why don't you do boots, and I'll do slacks.

Beat.

Shall we have boots here, and slacks over there like before?

LEAH *goes to the corner and starts lining up the boots*.

Two boots per person, Leah, remember?

LEAH *puts two boots together*.

One left. One right.

LEAH *checks and swaps the boots*.

That's it. Good girl.

(*To* BETH.) What's your name? Can you tell me your name?

BETH. Beth.

MMOMA. Your name is Beth.

BETH. My name is Beth.

MMOMA. Beth, can you do something for me? Can you bag up buttons for me? I'm going to give you loose buttons, and you're going to sort them into regiment. Can you do that, Beth? Can you do that for me?

BETH *nods*.

All right then.

Everybody look where you are for buttons. Whatever buttons you can find in ten seconds and we're going to give those buttons to Beth, okay? Ready?

Ten. Nine. Eight.

MMOMA, LEAH *and* BETH *search for buttons.*

Seven. Six. Five.

All the women stop. They breathe in and out.

Four. Three.

They resume the search.

Two. One.

The women turn to her with handfuls of buttons.

Now give me all your buttons, and we'll sort them into regiment.

The women collect all the buttons together and settle down for the sorting.

The End.

Other Plays for Young People to Perform from Nick Hern Books

Original Plays

13
Mike Bartlett

100
Christopher Heimann,
Neil Monaghan, Diene Petterle

BLOOD AND ICE
Liz Lochhead

BLUE STOCKINGS
Jessica Swale

BOYS
Ella Hickson

BUNNY
Jack Thorne

BURYING YOUR BROTHER IN THE
  PAVEMENT
Jack Thorne

CHRISTMAS IS MILES AWAY
Chloë Moss

DISCO PIGS
Enda Walsh

EARTHQUAKES IN LONDON
Mike Bartlett

EIGHT
Ella Hickson

GIRLS LIKE THAT
Evan Placey

HOW TO DISAPPEAR COMPLETELY
  AND NEVER BE FOUND
Fin Kennedy

I CAUGHT CRABS IN WALBERSWICK
Joel Horwood

KINDERTRANSPORT
Diane Samuels

MOGADISHU
Vivienne Franzmann

MOTH
Declan Greene

THE MYSTAE
Nick Whitby

OVERSPILL
Ali Taylor

PRONOUN
Evan Placey

SAME
Deborah Bruce

THERE IS A WAR
Tom Basden

THE URBAN GIRL'S GUIDE TO
  CAMPING AND OTHER PLAYS
Fin Kennedy

THE WARDROBE
Sam Holcroft

Adaptations

ANIMAL FARM
Ian Wooldridge
Adapted from George Orwell

ARABIAN NIGHTS
Dominic Cooke

BEAUTY AND THE BEAST
Laurence Boswell

CORAM BOY
Helen Edmundson
Adapted from Jamila Gavin

DAVID COPPERFIELD
Alastair Cording
Adapted from Charles Dickens

GREAT EXPECTATIONS
Nick Ormerod and Declan Donnellan
Adapted from Charles Dickens

HIS DARK MATERIALS
Nicholas Wright
Adapted from Philip Pullman

THE JUNGLE BOOK
Stuart Paterson
Adapted from Rudyard Kipling

KENSUKE'S KINGDOM
Stuart Paterson
Adapted from Michael Morpurgo

KES
Lawrence Till
Adapted from Barry Hines

THE LOTTIE PROJECT
Vicky Ireland
Adapted from Jacqueline Wilson

MIDNIGHT
Vicky Ireland
Adapted from Jacqueline Wilson

NOUGHTS & CROSSES
Dominic Cooke
Adapted from Malorie Blackman

THE RAILWAY CHILDREN
Mike Kenny
Adapted from E. Nesbit

SWALLOWS AND AMAZONS
Helen Edmundson and Neil Hannon
Adapted from Arthur Ransome

TO SIR, WITH LOVE
Ayub Khan-Din
Adapted from E.R Braithwaite

TREASURE ISLAND
Stuart Paterson
Adapted from Robert Louis Stevenson

WENDY & PETER PAN
Ella Hickson
Adapted from J.M. Barrie

THE WOLVES OF WILLOUGHBY
  CHASE
Russ Tunney
Adapted from Joan Aiken

For more information on plays to perform visit
www.nickhernbooks.co.uk/plays-to-perform

www.nickhernbooks.co.uk

 facebook.com/nickhernbooks

 twitter.com/nickhernbooks